DATE DUE			

921
SOU

Cu|

3 24571 0900466 7
Wells, PeggySue.

Soulja Boy Tell 'Em

CPS-MORRILL ES
CHICAGO PUBLIC SCHOOLS
6011 S ROCKWELL ST
CHICAGO, IL 60629

349442 01850   32744B   0001

Blue Banner Biography

Soulja Boy Tell 'Em

PeggySue Wells

P.O. Box 196
Hockessin, Delaware 19707
Visit us on the web: www.mitchelllane.com
Comments? email us: mitchelllane@mitchelllane.com

Mitchell Lane **PUBLISHERS**

Printing   2   3   4   5   6   7   8   9

Blue Banner Biographies

Akon	Alan Jackson	Alicia Keys
Allen Iverson	Ashanti	Ashlee Simpson
Ashton Kutcher	Avril Lavigne	Bernie Mac
Beyoncé	Bow Wow	Brett Favre
Britney Spears	Carrie Underwood	Chris Brown
Chris Daughtry	Christina Aguilera	Christopher Paul Curtis
Ciara	Clay Aiken	Condoleezza Rice
Corbin Bleu	Daniel Radcliffe	David Ortiz
Derek Jeter	Eminem	Eve
Fergie (Stacy Ferguson)	50 Cent	Gwen Stefani
Ice Cube	Jamie Foxx	Ja Rule
Jay-Z	Jennifer Lopez	Jessica Simpson
J. K. Rowling	Johnny Depp	JoJo
Justin Berfield	Justin Timberlake	Kanye West
Kate Hudson	Keith Urban	Kelly Clarkson
Kenny Chesney	Lance Armstrong	Lindsay Lohan
Mariah Carey	Mario	Mary J. Blige
Mary-Kate and Ashley Olsen	Michael Jackson	Miguel Tejada
Missy Elliott	Nancy Pelosi	Nelly
Orlando Bloom	P. Diddy	Paris Hilton
Peyton Manning	Queen Latifah	Rihanna
Ron Howard	Rudy Giuliani	Sally Field
Sean Kingston	Selena	Shakira
Shirley Temple	**Soulja Boy Tell 'Em**	Taylor Swift
Timbaland	Tim McGraw	Toby Keith
Usher	Vanessa Anne Hudgens	Zac Efron

Library of Congress Cataloging-in-Publication Data
Wells, PeggySue.
Soulja Boy Tell 'Em / by PeggySue Wells.
    p. cm. — (Blue banner biographies)
Includes bibliographical references, discography, and index.
ISBN 978-1-58415-676-5 (library bound)
1. Soulja Boy, 1990– — Juvenile literature. 2. Rap musicians — United States — Biography — Juvenile literature. I. Title.
ML3930.S69W45 2009
782.421649092 — dc22
[B]

2008008062

ABOUT THE AUTHOR: PeggySue Wells is the author of many books, including the *What to Do When . . .* series and, for Mitchell Lane Publishers, *Fergie* and *Kanye West*. A popular speaker, she has written screenplays, books, and curriculum. Her magazine articles appear nationally. She's a member of the Remedy.FM advisory board and the Christian Performing Arts Fellowship, and is a coordinator for the Tweener Ministries international teen writing competition. Wells is the proud mother of seven children. For more information, visit her web site, PeggySueWells.com.

PUBLISHER'S NOTE: The following story has been thoroughly researched, and to the best of our knowledge represents a true story. While every possible effort has been made to ensure accuracy, the publisher will not assume liability for damages caused by inaccuracies in the data, and makes no warranty on the accuracy of the information contained herein. This story has not been authorized or endorsed by Soulja Boy Tell 'Em.

Blue Banner Biography

Grammy nominee for Best Rap Song, DeAndre "Soulja Boy Tell 'Em" Way attended the 50th Annual Grammy Awards held in Los Angeles on February 10, 2008.

A Movement Begins

*F*rom the shoes he wears to the shades and the rubber band necklace, Soulja Boy has designed his own movement. Initially wearing oversized shirts and brightly colored sneakers decorated with star lightning bolts, the young singer hit the stage with his own songs and dance moves. Later performances were done shirtless, with his pants pulled way below the waistband of his underwear. "Different cities like different songs," he described. "Different crowds do different dances. But so far everyone shows me love. Doing shows is what I love to do."

He was still a teenager when DeAndre Way, commonly known as Soulja Boy Tell 'Em, was recognized as a businessman, producer, hitmaker, and entertainer.

"Before I was rapping, I was just a regular kid in school," he said. "I just liked to chill with my friends and play games and stuff like that. One day at school my friends were freestyling at the lunch table and that's where it all started."

Disc jockey and producer Mr. Collipark accompanied DeAndre to the 2007 BET Hip Hop Awards at the Atlanta Civic Center.

When he was in high school, DeAndre signed with manager Michael Crooms, known as Mr. Collipark. "He's already seen my fan base and my following," DeAndre said. "He told me, 'Do everything how you've been doing it, and I'm gonna just sit back and let you do you. I'm a let you go in the studio and do you, and when you're finished, turn in your album. You've proven yourself. If it's not broke, don't fix it. You've already proven that this is what the people want to hear, so do what you've been doing."

The Associated Press reported, "Soulja Boy created the number one pop sensation of 2007—'Crank Dat (Soulja Boy).' " Hitting the radio in May of that year, "Crank Dat" rocketed to number one on Billboard's Hot 100 in September, scored as a number one ringtone, and number one on iTunes. Soulja Boy's video stream for "Crank Dat" grabbed the number 26 spot.

"It wasn't just to have fame or whatever. I just wanted to have everybody jumpin' in the party."

"Music was at the core of everything we did in 2007," said Van Toffler, President of MTV Networks' Music Group. "And, once again, MTV, VH1, and CMT [Country Music Television] produced the year's most memorable events in music." On that list, "Crank Dat" ranked above Alicia Keys's "No One" at 28, Kanye West's "Stronger" at number 29, and Beyoncé's "Get Me Bodied" at number 30.

"It was just something I was doing," DeAndre said. "It wasn't just to have fame or whatever. I just wanted to have everybody jumpin' in the party. When I hit a party, I'd be putting my CD in and everybody would go ahead and 'Crank It Up.' That's what it was about. But as far as the point I'm at now, I [didn't] know it was ever gonna be this big. I'm on a whole 'nother level."

For the 50th Annual Grammy Awards, Soulja Boy Tell 'Em's "Crank Dat" received the nomination for the 2007 Best Rap song.

"He's the best," Mr. Collipark stated. "He out-hustled these cats. He out-thinks these cats. He's out-performing these cats. And he's so young. He was sixteen when I found him. He don't even have the vocabulary to be competing with these cats. At a time when the game is so messed up, there are very few success stories in rap music right now and he's one of them. And he's winning big. So you gotta give credit to that."

"I don't respond to skepticism because they not gonna be skeptical for long."

"I'm different, in terms of my style, what I rap about, what I do, how I do it, the way I put it together. I switch up doing comedy, the snap, the dance, the party, the happy, the sad, all of that," DeAndre described. "I don't respond to skepticism because they not gonna be skeptical for long. My life right now is like a TV show; you watch every day to see a new episode. They waiting to see what I'm [gonna] do next."

Southern Roots

*D*eAndre Cortez Way was born July 28, 1990, in Chicago, Illinois. He is better known by his stage name, Soulja Boy Tell 'Em. An American rapper, he was originally known simply as Soulja Boy, until copyright issues interfered. Claiming he first created the stage name Souljah Boy, with an *h*, William Lyons of the Home Dogs sued DeAndre on December 9, 2007. DeAndre adjusted his name to Soulja Boy Tell 'Em.

When he was six years old, DeAndre moved with his family to Atlanta, Georgia, a city that was becoming a hotbed for music. "I didn't like growing up, we were poor," he said. "When I was staying with my momma, it was me and my little brother. We didn't have much money. I ain't have nothing to do, just go to school. I used to be real smart, a straight-A student. But music affected my grades, I ain't gonna lie."

In the South, he developed a love for rap music. "It's controversial because people saying the South killing hip-hop, but I feel it's new and different, and people still stuck on the old stuff," he observed. "It's changing. I'm fitting to be the next generation."

He partnered with Young Kwon, who taught him how to make repetitive beats, saying the same thing over and over. "He was the one who taught me how to make beats and records; he recorded the first songs I ever did," DeAndre said. "He taught me what he knew about snap beats in the studio in his house."

> "I took the hood to where the money was at. If I didn't have no money behind it, nobody would've ever known about it."

In eighth grade, DeAndre moved with his father to Batesville, Mississippi, a town with a population of about 8,000. His father bought him his first computer. "I moved with my daddy because he had a little money, he could provide more for me," DeAndre said. "That's where I got access to a computer. It got me where I am."

The new location provided new opportunities. "When I went to Mississippi, I had to adjust to what was going on," he described. "But it was really a blessing in disguise because if I would've never moved to Mississippi, I wouldn't be where I am today. I wouldn't have had access to no computer, no Internet and no camera to film my dancing. I took the hood to where the money was at. If I didn't have no money behind it, nobody would've ever known about it."

Sporting his trademark bright colors and ball cap, DeAndre was a guest at the 2nd Annual Ozone Magazine Awards. The magazine published a feature on the young artist.

While plenty of famous people say they became an overnight success after ten years of working for it, DeAndre's move to popularity was meteoric. Going from a kid to a Grammy Award nominee was a short two-year trip for him.

In 2004, DeAndre returned to Atlanta. "When I moved back to Atlanta, I was like, 'I gotta get my momma out of this right here," he said. "Then my career started to jump off, and the money started coming in."

In November of 2005, DeAndre posted his songs on SoundClick, an online music-based social community. "First we uploaded songs to SoundClick, where people can comment on your songs, rate them, and download them," he explained. "We were getting good responses, so I set up my website, www.souljaboytellem.com, to help push my name."

Borrowing his cousin's video camera, DeAndre taped videos of himself and friends doing popular teen dances. He uploaded these videos onto the Internet. "I don't think it's just the music," he said. "I think it's me that people like. My personality come through, and my style. I think somebody who just hears my music and doesn't know me won't like me as much as somebody who's seen me perform."

The teen collaborated with classmate Abraham Mustafa, called Arab, to form the duo the 30/30 Boys. Michael Sykes, known as M.I.A.M.I. (Money Isn't A Major Issue) Mike,

> *"I don't think it's just the music. . . . I think it's me that people like. My personality come through, and my style."*

Abraham "Arab" Mustafa (left) and DeAndre began making music together in their early teens, traveling and performing in concerts together.

managed the boys. "I started the company Stacks On Deck Entertainment by myself," DeAndre said. "Once I did that, M.I.A.M.I. Mike heard of me from the Internet and from me doing little shows in Mississippi. M.I.A.M.I. Mike has helped me out a lot in the streets; that's where I was lacking."

DeAndre traveled to Indianapolis, Indiana, when he was fifteen for his first live performance at a teen nightclub. "The first time I stepped onstage was wild," he recalled. "The show was so crunk that I was worried about doing a whack show. But then I just calmed down and did it."

On January 13, 2006, DeAndre opened a YouTube account, where, he says, "people can put your face to the things you spitting."

One month later, in February of 2006, DeAndre moved onto MySpace. More people heard his music, and his fan base increased. The next year, in February 2007, he released an independent album, *Unsigned and Still Major.* In March of 2007, he recorded "Crank Dat." The next month, on April 11, DeAndre was the subject of a low-budget video that showed the "Crank Dat" dance steps, which was played on YouTube. In May, "Crank Dat" received its first commercial radio airplay.

> *"He hit me on my Sidekick and gave me a number to call. . . . I hit him up and I signed with him that same week."*

Next, DeAndre paired up with Atlanta-based manager Mr. Collipark of the Collipark Music imprint. "I've always been rapping," he said, "so back in school everybody knew me as Soulja Boy. I always had songs out and I had a couple local hits or whatever, so I was signing autographs and stuff back before I signed my record deal when I was just in high school."

Collipark met with DeAndre in May and offered him a contract. The teenager signed. "He hit me on my Sidekick and gave me a number to call," DeAndre recalled. "I hit him up and I signed with him that same week. He signed me in my house, in my living room. Then I went to L.A. and I signed with Interscope."

On August 12, 2007, "Crank Dat" appeared on *Entourage,* an Emmy Award–winning HBO series. The next month, the song placed in the top ten of Billboard's Hot 100. "Crank Dat" also topped the list of Billboard's RingMasters chart.

Using the demo version of FL Studio, a digital recording program, DeAndre produced his entire album, *Souljaboytellem.com*. (FL Studios continues to offer a demonstration version of their software, but users can no longer save the work they produce with the demo.) This second album was released in October 2007.

As a high school senior, DeAndre combined his studies with his career as a rapper, touring with a tutor. His album, *Souljaboytellem. com*, did not sell very well, but the single "Crank Dat" became an Internet phenomenon. It sold well as a single and as a ringtone.

DeAndre listed 50 Cent as one of his influences. "I might not rap like him. But this man has movies, video games, 11-times-platinum albums, clothes, shoes, drinks. . . . I could go on all day. That is my biggest inspiration. I just keep it in my mind. If he can do it, I can too."

But not everyone was thrilled with DeAndre's quick success. He received plenty of criticism from a variety of sources.

"That is my biggest inspiration. I just keep it in my mind. If [50 Cent] can do it, I can too."

Harnessing the Internet

*I*n 2006, DeAndre's MySpace page generated millions of reviews and broke the site's record.

"The Internet had been a big help with my career," he said. "My advice to musicians, Internet is the key. It gets your music heard all across the world."

In contrast to the vast number of musicians who posted their work on MySpace and YouTube, DeAndre implemented a strategy that got the attention of millions of viewers. "When I started recording songs, I wasn't getting no love from the radio stations or DJs. I was a nobody," he said. "So when I recorded 'Crank Dat (Superman),' I'd take whatever was the number one song in the country at the time or the song everybody was listening to that was on BET—like 50 Cent's 'In Da Club,' for example, that was a huge record. Everybody was downloading music for free off the Internet and there's websites where everybody goes to get new music.

So when I recorded 'Crank Dat (Superman),' I'd rename it '50 Cent—In Da Club' and I'd upload it to where people could download it for free. Then I'd copy it and rename it as a Justin Timberlake song, a Master P song, a Jay-Z song; every big artist you could think of. So every time you got on that site and tried to download a 50 Cent song or a Jay-Z song, you'd get the 'Crank Dat' record. Everybody was like, 'Who is this dude right here?' " While some people question the ethics of riding on the names and fame of other artists, song titles are not under copyright law.

In addition to publishing his music on the Internet, DeAndre uploaded over 100 dance videos. The Internet served as a two-way communication between DeAndre and his growing fan base. When he posted easy-to-do dance steps for "Crank Dat," the movements became the biggest dance sensation since the Macarena of the early 1990s. The video was filmed in the same empty swimming pool featured in the 2007 film *Stomp the Yard.*

When he posted easy-to-do dance steps for "Crank Dat," the movements became the biggest dance sensation since the Macarena.

"Everybody was trying to learn the dance, but nobody really knew how to do it right," DeAndre said.

By the end of 2007, the YouTube "Crank Dat" instructional video, in which DeAndre breaks down each move, had received more than 21 million hits. The single's music video had received more than 25 million views.

DeAndre taught his "Crank Dat" dance steps to actress Natalie Portman on a New York stage, and to his fans nationwide via an instructional video he uploaded on the Internet.

"Ah, man, it was just something I was doing in the bedroom of my house and having fun," DeAndre said. "I'm surprised it got this big."

And people responded. More than 40,000 homemade video clips of people from all walks of life dancing to "Crank Dat" were posted on the Internet. Even clips from animated shows were looped to make it look as if the characters cranked, including Bambi, Barney, Dora the Explorer, the Lion King, the Simpsons, and SpongeBob SquarePants.

Convergence Culture Consortium reported, "The whole thing snowballed until people like Beyoncé started incorporating the dance into her stage show. By that point, everyone from underground rap magazines to *The Atlantic* was talking about Soulja Boy. Beyond the novelty of seeing everyone from Winnie the Pooh to a bunch of vaguely coordinated MIT students doing the 'Crank That' dance, the rise of Soulja Boy is an interesting exploration of self-promotion in the digital landscape."

The infectious tune and video spawned a wildly popular dance fad. As the buzz for "Crank Dat" spread from the Internet to the streets, kids were talking about it at the park where Michael Crooms' sons played. Crooms, known for his work in producing the Ying Yang Twins and Young Jeezy, heard about DeAndre from kids at the park and signed the teenager to a major-label contract with Interscope Records.

While the Internet proved the vehicle to make DeAndre's work a household phenomenon, it also allowed consumers to get his music for free. "The only thing you can do about that is capitalize on it," DeAndre said. "Instead of selling 50,000 [albums] your first week and no ringtones, if you sell 50,000 your first week and four million ringtones, you're straight. So capitalize on the digital market. Don't fight against it or you ain't gonna have no money."

"So capitalize on the digital market. Don't fight against it or you ain't gonna have no money."

Criticism

*C*onsidered a crunk and snap music rap artist from the South, DeAndre was the target of criticism from both reviewers and fellow rappers who have been in the business for a long time. The complaints leveled at the young rapper's style maintained that the lyrical content was low, without real meaning or purpose.

Rapper Jermaine Dupri commented, "It makes the record companies not want to artist-develop the groups anymore because that's what they're into—they want to try and sell as many ringtones as possible."

"They're not making substance material—they're not really going into creating a sound. It's all about making the hot song for right now, but the artists who will stand the test of time like myself are about making records, not songs," Snoop Dogg said. "You got to make a quality album so you can hold people's attention. It's like a movie. If you make a movie that got [only] one good scene, ain't nobody gonna go see it."

Veteran rapper 50 Cent said, "Right now the state of where we are at in hip-hop, it's different. I don't think they want the lyrics to be complex—they want it to be simple, catchy. The Southern-based artist can be credited [with] that, because they're dancing, so now your record has to pretty much be catchy. It doesn't have to be super content, extreme content. It has to have a good rhythm to it and dance."

DeAndre believed that lyrical complexity and high content in his songs was not what his fans were buying. "People don't want to go to a club and hear [about] people getting shot or hear about your life story," he said. "People want to . . . have fun and dance and party."

Members of the "hip-hop is dead" group labeled "Crank Dat" as "ringtone rap." They accused DeAndre of not living up to the style of the genre's great artists of the past. Reviews in *Entertainment Weekly* described "Crank Dat" as "a teenage wasteland filled with monotony looped chants and agonizing blunt-force beats."

"I don't care about reviews, I care about sales," DeAndre responded. "As long as my album sells more than the other rapper, it's all good. As long as my fans are happy, I'm straight. I don't make music to make the critics happy 'cause they're not gonna be happy anyway. I make music to please my fan base who's been down with me before the deal."

> "I don't make music to make the critics happy 'cause they're not gonna be happy anyway. I make music to please my fan base."

Despite the criticism from fellow rappers and music critics, no one can argue that DeAndre dominated the 2007 hip-hop scene. "Love it or loathe it, 'Crank Dat (Soulja Boy)' is the biggest pop novelty of 2007, and only partly because it was the country's number one single for seven weeks this fall," wrote Richard Harrington of the *Washington Post*. In its first week, *Souljaboytellem.com* sold 117,000 copies and debuted at number four on the Billboard 200. By March 2008, the album had sold over 826,000 copies.

"I wasn't making it for everybody to like me," DeAndre said. "Now a lot of people hate that song and a lot of people love it, so it's just crazy. They like the beat, they like the song and they like the dance. It's not like something separate, and it's not something you got to sit down and take time to learn."

Despite its popularity, "Crank Dat" has been banned at some school dances and skating rinks for sexual slang and innuendo.

DeAndre wasn't fazed by the critics. "It's rhythm, man," he said. "It's action-packed, it's crunk. When the beat comes on, it just makes you wanna move. If not, [you're] dead."

From the beginning, the teen rapper held a firm philosophy regarding criticism. "I really don't care what people think. That's where most rappers mess up," he stated. "I had the number one song in the country seven weeks straight and sold over three million ringtones. I've had critics all my life. When I first started doing my

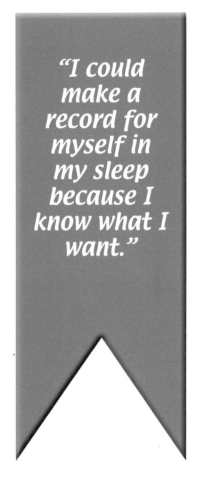

"I could make a record for myself in my sleep because I know what I want."

shades in high school, I had written 'Soulja Boy' on them in [correction fluid] and everybody was talkin' about me like, 'Man, that's stupid.' Today, I'm selling a hundred pair of 'em a day on SouljaBoyTellem.com. So when I sit back and think about it, man, I don't really care what nobody says."

Moving Forward

*A*s a savvy businessman, DeAndre had big plans for the future and a finger on the pulse of the music industry's direction. After traveling with a tutor as a high school senior, DeAndre received his diploma. "We did a back-to-school special with BET and I went back to my high school and all my teachers and the principal were tellin' 'em my situation, letting all my fans out there know how it all went down with my education," DeAndre said. "I went back to my 'hood and everybody was like, 'Soulja Boy! Soulja Boy!' Once you make it out of the 'hood, you're the person everybody looks up to."

Even before his fame, DeAndre had a list of what he wanted to accomplish and has been on a fast track to get there. "I always look at it like, this is just something else I want to do," he described. "This ain't really nothin', you know? It's just having a goal or an accomplishment or something that you want to do. I wanted to have the number one song in the country and now I've done that. I want to have a platinum-selling album and I'm still working on that."

DeAndre continues to grow and develop as an artist. "He learns so quick. He asks a lot of questions and he observes a lot," Crooms said. "He's a student of music. Anytime you got an artist that produces himself, that does his own beats and puts songs together like that, it's something special about him. And he's able to go in and make records. There's a lot of artists that can't make records. He's a young Kanye in his world. If you look at the variety of subject matters, the lifestyle records that he put together, they're very primitive, but it's a lifestyle thing that he's done with [his singles] the 'Bapes,' the 'Yahh,' the 'Crank Dat,' the 'Shoot Out,' the 'Just Got My Report Card.' It's a bunch of different themes that appeal to those kids. So as he grows and the things that he sees expands, he'll be making records about that stuff."

"I still wanna have my own cartoon and I'm trying to do that," DeAndre said, listing his dreams. "I want to be in a movie so I'm gonna do that. It's just something else to do, so there's no reason to get big-headed from it because it could be gone tomorrow. Plus, whoever's hot, you're not gonna be able to do this forever. When you're hot, you're hot and when you're not, you're not. All this could be gone tomorrow."

> "It's just something else to do, so there's no reason to get big-headed from it because it could be gone tomorrow."

In a rare departure from his signature oversized clothes and self-styled jewelry, DeAndre wore a suit and tie to the November 2007 American Music Awards in Los Angeles.

In the initial stages, DeAndre's friend Arab did the illustrations for the cartoon project. "The cartoon is called *Bad Lil' Homiez*," he said. "It's really based on my life, with a twist to it. I'm gonna have superpowers. It's funny though, it's not too kiddy and it's not too grown. It's for everybody."

Venturing into other areas of entertainment, DeAndre revealed in 2007, "I've been out to L.A. and I met with Nickelodeon, Disney, Paramount Pictures, and a lot of casting directors to do auditions. So y'all might see Soulja Boy Tell 'Em on the big screen [soon]."

DeAndre produced Arab on his Stacks On Deck Entertainment label and is expanding the label by

His own best marketer, by age seventeen DeAndre had already scored a number one hit on Billboard's Top 100 and launched a wildly popular YouTube dance fad with "Crank Dat (Superman)."

introducing fresh new artists. "I think everything is gonna go digital," he predicted. "I don't think there's gonna be any more albums being sold. You know how they had the eight-track and then that went away? Then they had the cassette tape, and then that went away and they had CDs. I think CDs are gonna die out, too, and they're gonna just have iTunes. Everything's gonna go digital. Ain't nobody gonna buy albums no more."

DeAndre is clear about what he is trying to accomplish with his music. "I'm trying to prove everybody wrong whoever told me I couldn't make it," he said. "To all the haters who say I can't rap and I will never make it, I'm going to show them. I make music for the crowd to dance and get crunk to. I make my tracks from the heart. And I think I'm bringing that new super fresh style to the game that don't nobody got yet. I see they snappin' and dancing. But I got that super fresh style to top it off. So I'm coming. Just watch me!"

"I make my tracks from the heart. . . . I got that super fresh style to top it off. So I'm coming. Just watch me!"

1990   DeAndre Cortez Way is born on July 28 in Chicago, Illinois.

1996   DeAndre and his mother move to Atlanta, Georgia.

2003   DeAndre relocates with his father to Batesville, Mississippi.

2004   Back in Atlanta, DeAndre establishes his Stacks On Deck Entertainment label.

2005   DeAndre posts his songs on SoundClick.

2006   DeAndre opens a YouTube account and expands onto MySpace.

2007   "Crank Dat" is recorded and released on his first independent album, *Unsigned and Still Major*. "Crank Dat" gets its first airplay. Mr. Collipark signs DeAndre to Interscope Records. "Crank Dat" appears on *Entourage* on HBO, Billboard's Hot 100, and Billboard's Hot RingMasters chart. It is nominated for Best Rap Song for the 50th Annual Grammy Awards. His second album, *Souljaboytellem.com*, is released in October.

2008   By March, Souljaboytellem.com has sold 826,000 copies in the United States, according to Nielsen SoundScan. In December, he releases *iSouljaBoyTellem*, which includes the hits "Birdwalk," "Kiss Me Thru the Phone," and "Turn My Swag On."

2009   He produces songs with Kanye West, Rihanna, Jamie Foxx, Fergie, and others, and he prepares his third studio album, *The DeAndre Way*, scheduled for release in 2010.

DISCOGRAPHY

Albums
2008   *iSouljaBoyTellem*
2007   *Souljaboytellem.com*
2007   *Unsigned & Still Major: Da Album Before Da Album*

Books

While there are no other books about Soulja Boy Tell 'Em written for young readers, you might enjoy the following Blue Banner Biographies of other urban artists:

Bankston, John. *Eminem.* Hockessin, Delaware: Mitchell Lane Publishers, 2004.

Boone, Mary. *50 Cent.* Hockessin, Delaware: Mitchell Lane Publishers, 2007.

———. *Akon.* Hockessin, Delaware: Mitchell Lane Publishers, 2008.

Torres, Jennifer. *Mary J. Blige.* Hockessin, Delaware: Mitchell Lane Publishers, 2008.

———. *Usher.* Hockessin, Delaware: Mitchell Lane Publishers, 2006.

Tracy, Kathleen. *Chris Brown.* Hockessin, Delaware: Mitchell Lane Publishers, 2008.

Works Consulted

Beverly, Julia. "Soulja Boy." *Ozone Magazine.* January 2008.

Cordor, Cyril. "Soulja Boy Tell 'Em Biography." *AOLMusic. com.* http://music.aol.com/artist/soulja-boy-tell-em/biography/667712

Crosley, Hillary. "Soulja Boy Hitting the Road with Lil' Mama." March, 17, 2008. *Billboard.com.* http://www.billboard.com/bbcom/news/article_display.jsp?vnu_content_id=1003726677

Harrington, Richard. "Web Cranks Soulja Boy." *Washington Post.* Associated Press, *Journal Gazette.* January 5, 2008.

Li, Xiaochang. "Hustling 2.0: Soulja Boy and the Crank Dat Phenomenon." *Convergence Culture Consortium: Comparative Media Studies at MIT.* October 9, 2007.

PR Newswire. "Driven by Music, MTV.com, VH1.com and CMT.com Deliver 1.2 Billion Video Streams in 2007: Women Ruled, Country Crossed Over and VMA Artists Rocked in MTV Networks Music Group's Top 30 Most-Streamed Music Videos of 2007." *CNN Money.com.* December 27, 2007,

"Soulja Boy — Biography." *LetsSingIt.com.* October, 17, 2007.
http://artists.letssingit.com/soulja-boy-7kp6l/biography

Underground Rap Scene. Interviews. "Soulja Boy."
http://Undergroundrapscene.com./Soulja_Boy_Interview.html

Vozick-Levinson, Simon. *"Souljaboytellem.com."* Music Review, *Entertainment Weekly,* October 5, 2007.
http://www.ew.com/ew/article/0,,20144964,00.html

On the Internet

Soulja Boy Tell 'Em Official Site
Souljaboytellem.com

Soulja Boy Tell 'Em's Official SoundClick
http://www.soundclick.com/members/default.cfm?member=Soulja-Boy

Soulja Boy Tell 'Em at MySpace
http://www.myspace.com/souljaboytellem

Soulja Boy Tell 'Em's YouTube channel
http://www.youtube.com/SouljaBoy